Strange Fruit

Kamau Brathwaite

Strange Fruit

PEEPAL TREE

Published in Great Britain in 2016 by
Peepal Tree Press Ltd
17 King's Avenue
Leeds LS6 1QS
England

Supported using public funding by
ARTS COUNCIL
ENGLAND

Strange Fruit

How cultural lynchin mek the deads
re. enter some of our poem (s)

Southern tree(s) bear(s) a strange fruit
Blood on the leaves & blood at the root
Black bodies swingin in the southern breeze
Strange fruit hanging from the poplar trees

Pastoral scene of the gallant South
The bulging eyes & the twisted mouth
Scent of magnolia sweet & fresh
Then the sudden smell of burning flesh

Here is a fruit for the crows to pluck
for the rain to gather
for the wind to suck
for the sun to rot
for the tree to drop
Here is a strange & bitter crop

Strange Fruit

<Lewis Allen=Abel Meeropol <1937>) . Billie Holiday from Commodore 78 rpm recording NYC 1939>

'When people are in danger, everyone has a duty to speak out.
No one has the right to pass by on the other side.'

- Kofi Annan -

Strange Fruit

She Poems

Icons & livications

Sperrits

End Poem Poens

The lynching Tree

from a position up to 2008 of good health. considerable energy. 'popularity'. productivity. suc-
cess – teaching two full classes (graduate/undergraduate) every semester. producing – among oth
ers - **Ancestors** (2001). the 2-vol **MR/MR** (2002). **Golokwati** (2002). **Ark** (2004). <u>G/2</u> 2 vols. <u>Eman-
cipation Anthology</u> 2 vols. **DS(2)** (2007). **Slow Horses** (2005). **Elegguas** (2010). working on new
projects in **MR** (inc concepts of *Radiance. Spiritual Realism. Xtreme Lyric.* the aesthetics of vodoun
[Dahomey-Haiti] as a response/talisman to New World Slavery . planning (an aborted!) <u>200th-An-</u>
<u>niversary of the Abolition of the Slave Trade Conference</u> (2007). the putting on our annual end-

of-semester (lass lap) student-public MARASSA since 1990. . . receiving some 40+ national regio-
nal & international invitations (mainly Africa the UK & Europe) to help blow the trumpet of my 80th
b/day 2010 and my work generally - but to which. by this time. i'm too bloody. weak & under-
drone to attend. . .and w/in a few months after this am i set sail in a frail craft back to a ship->
wreck on my island of Barabados. . .

T[i]

his poem – *series of MESONGS really* – start wid dis TEEFIN – for years an-

years since c2004 the surgically selected removal from our apartment of
our spiritual possessions - the books & archives artifacts that make up the
story of my life – creating(!) all else that follows - induced loneliness & i->
solation. the desolation of betrayal. that spinal tingle of unease of unre->
Quited LOSS. trauma of underthrow of all i have been doing fought for/to-
wards and stood for - And here comes this huge sophisticated apparatus
of sharade designed to destroy my life - its participatory xpressioning of <<
an alternative – *alter/native nativist* – cosmology - 'alter/native' only be-<
cause of having to fight for/define/maintain its own space of valida-
tion because iT represents THE OTHER - other gods & language Other
challenges & chalices - the capsule not the missile[1] - sycoraX and >
NOT the Planter Plantation Playwrite Prospero. and for witch the TARGET

---

[1] see **Missile & Capsule** (SavacouNorth 2004)

/victim/violin - **is played upon the block – the auction tree** of physical and psycho-cultural lynching & the whole mad made to seem – *w/out invention/intervention from the Authorities* - '**miraculous**' or *poltergeist* - an INSIDE JOB (in < both *senses* of the novel) - **as if it didn't happen in my flesh but only in the wic-(k)ed fish & spirit of my poor 'imagination'** . **So NObody is RESPONS. ABLE – dem look-way. look-the-other-way. dem pass-by on the other side**

So since. strangely . no one is speakin out -- it is **>** this (unXpected) **inSINeration that i've had DEFEND myself – even unto the embarrassment** - in a way - of having to write this INTRODUCTION of 'historical record' - *as if i've done >* somebody/something wrong & have to xplain/*apologize* for these GOINGS-ON – as if my MURDER - the teefin of my HEALTH & HAIR & HERITAGE . loss of my JOB *as part/result of this & therefore my* CONTRIBUTION-SHARING-<< TEACHING-LEARNING-EARNINGS-WRITING – my present past + FUTURE GAAN – th -is new deep HOLE or MESON[2] from which there seems no MEDICAL progno-sis/resolution[3]. no SECURITY/FORENSIC INVESTIGATION[4]. LEGAL AID/redress < in JUSTICE from the ole piracy of my ID BIRTH PASSPORT MARRIAGE PROP-ERTY CERFITICATES PHOTOS my MOTHER's LETTERS WORKBOXES of RESEAR-CH and my OWN WRITING since 1950 . my few vertiginous secrets like in < my private papers love-letters/letters (since they have access to EVERYWHERE) sha-

---

[2] KB uses two similar sounds in his recent work – *meson* = sargasso hole/blockage/entanglement of forces . *mesong* is the release from this. See **MR/MR** (SavacouNorth 2002. 2 vols)

[3] and the HEALTH itself might have recovered had not the TEEFIN gone on & on. . .for 8 years. . .2004-2011 – when dem throw i out

[4] but then mine wasn't that kind of murder.   i guess. . .

red now w/STRANGERS & those dangerous & unpredictable conSEQUENCes . theft from and SABOTAGE my sycoraX COMPUTERS . such AWEsome & All-seeing SURVEILLANCE – phone-tap & micro-camera – that if we left the apartment by itself for just 10 mins. you cd be SURE that if they wish or need it SOMETHING GONE and yet NO public or collegial or employer outCRY comment or concern ref the + 4000 items 'disappear'd' – as if my REFT & UNDERTHROW – remove from ACTIVE SERVICE! - is my own FRUIT & FANTASY & FAU -LT – yu had it comin to yu buddy! - scapegoat scapeghost and monkey-moko scarifice

i call this "CL" - CULTURAL LYNCHING – a psycho-physical cultural slip-knot assassination – a use > me of what Miss Afrika (Barbados prophet) calls 'a radio-active medallion" – or rather IMPLANT – a (successful) neurological & technological xperiment in post-9/11 metropolitan obeah - design not only to destroy my personal ACHIEVEMENT CONTRIBUTION but to mek me a BAD XAMPLE in the eyes of my own people who until this lynching wd have 'looked up to me' as a GOOD NEIGBOURLY XAMPLE of how we cd 'get along' w/Prospero – GOOD RODNEY KING & CALIBAN - now suddenly & un-Xplainably the OPPOSITE – somebody to be SHAME about – don't name yr chilldrens after - compleat disMANtellin the artist - the 'dis. appearance' of the mwe that use(d) to be - my whole fairweather world of marb-le-pitchin-ideas-friends & fela-sperrits gorne - neoCOLONIALISM w/a vengeance

---

5 AndrOid's (Jan 2011) ''Who doesn't want a Radioactive Medallion to hang around?'

Therefore am i now treated like a ghost or ghoul or leper - even by my own pe ople of the coral - like a shame & shambles. disappointment & dis. grace. th (e) kind of FAILURE they always talk about inside the rum-shop colony – the guy who goes to foreign like if he is a BIG-SHOTT until things go wrong an down > de hill e come an end-up back-home on the streets and left ABANDON in the dere liction of the SCARCECROW – warning fe those who think that Caliban & syco-> raX & Toussaint = smaddy. how dare yu challenge w/yr NATION-LANGUAGE' > de tap-natch status of the Prospero Plantation and ijs agent/agency THE BASILISK

So that NO ONE believe – evvabody totally PRETENN – that this down-cast and treason come to me as-man – as if i MEK MY OWN DESTRUCTION UP! – a > 'figment' in th mid-air-last-curve-contour my career and places me inside a cave or deep-hole-of-despond like some mad monk or hermit-pilgrim ship- wreck/castaway who gets no ECHO back to voices of his call for HELP from hell

The master-plan of the CL was/is to make it seem that the TEEFIN was/is a 'figment of my imagination' . that i was/am in fact suffering from a MAN- TAL PROBLEM – DEMENTIA - (something first 'reveal' to me by one of my MR students & repeated by a visiting Eng lit professor from the UK) – not only as rumoured or ar moured or enamoured 'fact'. but as STATISTICAL PROBABILITY & XPECTA-> TION – i'm then 81) – which is WHY i'm so easily misrepresented as re. TIRED >

---

[6] see **History of the Voice** (New Beacon 1984)

because of AGE *i* – this **RAGE** > mwe – aspects of **RACE** . offshoots of >

CULTURE CONFLICT at *so* many human – *purposeful & subliminal* – levels – cau-se i can't cope w/the teefin teefin teefin or rather my *imagination* of it – > And have remained in this 'imaginary' evva sence[7] And if this 'autosuggest-ion' doesn't work. they'll wait for the emergence of the more classic & ev entual aneurism heart-attack cancer or sleep apnea. like

Daniel in de Den

---

[7] Indeed there is *one* public comment & report – in the on-line Bajan Reporter 16+28 March 2010 which xpresses concern and carries a list of the first>>> STOLENS. But there is a cautionary note: 'We'd like to know are these items really stolen or just mis-placed? *Can another family member be holding them* to *store for safety?*' [AirBourne/bajanreporter.com/?p=9392. my emph]

That m'm able to continue work – from memory/from scratch! – but for how long?

– having been desTROY me root & branches

But even as i write – is like a flinger flickering a leaf or feather of the spirit w/the body lying dead along the other else of life that keeps the poetry << not poverty or scar but love and the continuation values even unto the grave to which i'm push . So note w/in this verse the reduce scale of prosody – the miniscule & tentative & scarred discovering tone – the use of Quiet clay & limestone - absence < of carnival & thronging congregations – xcept the sudden GLORIOUS moment of NOMMO REVELATION towards the end of 'Sperrits' (pp69-73) below. And of course there is the problem publication of my work since the CL programme. So much ERASURE. and even if a body wish . it will now be nigh impossible to write my history/bio graphy   like on the middlepassage

But i give Thanks & Praises for the sun & tune i nvr know was there aft->

er the 'great' choral voicings of the trilogies that prompt this trap to >
trip me up in this CATASTROPHE OF CRIPPLE DIS. CON-
TENT. which sun & tune itself is MIRACLE - these 55 mesongs i had <
nvr dream i own. written along the v/edge & coast of death & carrefour >
while almost blind & dumb & more house-bound *pyjamanero* every day – >
the conseQuence of something not my doin . and design to make me col-
ony & slave again but which i'll fight & fight > until i dead + dead to live
+ live again

Laura Nelson. at the beginning of this Tree. was. w/her 15 yr-old son. lynch from this bridge over the Canadian River Oklahoma
May 25 1911.   Laura can be clearly seen suspending over the water & reflexing in it in this postcardphotograph

Note

My longpoem response to my CL (cultural lynching) was immediate & persistent.
(1) **Dead Man Witness** [DMW] @ WSW [Washington sQuare West, NYC
Aug 2008 [unpub]. **(2)** **End Poem Poems** [EPP] @ WSW May 2011 [re-
jected by publisher]. (3) **Strange Fruit** @ WSW May 2011 and CowPastor [CP],
Barbados July 2012 [disQualified, as mss. by Casa de las Americas, as reQuirements
changed w/out my know- ledge. at last a publisher]. **(4)** **The Lazarus Poems** @ CP
May 2013 [im limbo w/publisher several years but winner Frank Collymore Award 2014].
(5) **eQuinox** @ CP Feb 2014 [accepted by publisher but since then under
reconsideration and prob gone thru de eddoes. . .]
(6) **Liviticus** @ CP March 2015. a publisher. **(7)** **Mercy Poems** @ CP May 2015.
(8) **Pentecostal Poems** @ CP Ap 2016

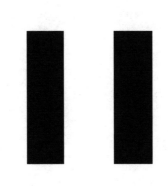

The Poems

»WSW«

The pictographs that follow xist of soiled & broken & disrupted souls

the evil spirits in these one-eyed owls
the loud howls of Fannie Lou

hammered in the Mississippi Transit Station trailer w/the name of Money
. Emmett Till . the muddy stain of memory inside the traitor cup w/out her womb
the river w/its nails their destiny

We live in Bagram every day. head in the bag at Abugrave

electrocuted on the auction block. yr hands
still in the gesture of committing peace like Christ the Buddha Gandhi reparation slaves

She sits bemurely in the darkened booth draped in its cloud of morning

There is a single flash of camera that clicks these poems' mourning

Basilisk

it's softer than a basilisk this basilisk
it doesn't have no shell
it comes from far down in the darkness
like from the ulcer depths of hell –
the radiation stepchile of a nuclear re-

actor in my head & balls & belly.   de-
voted to contamination downfall failure death
its two horns and its sense of double
which evva whe i shift & move & wangle
it brings me trouble

Sometime ago i don't kno when or how or why -
it born - probably in 9/11 –
in scorm & fear & hatred dread & terror racism –

one horn my friend the black .   my white friend
on the other .   like in the Nicolás Guillén poem .
like in plantation discourse .   creole criticism -

and because of this. both 'so-called'. neither
of them 'true'/'sincere' – both neither nvr you
both compromised corrupt
designed to disrupt peace the healthy breath of life

i plant a tree/you dig a hole a well . i gather up the plural fragrance
and you consume the whole .   one horn emblazon ribbon'd w/CP
the other mark CL which mek me sick and let me loose my job
. is how my latter life begin & end

And so you live me in
you germ yrself into my-
self & body spirit blood & bone

and you begin yr feeding on my soul
changing me dramatic from my intensive green to foul
from agile to this splinter like this thin-like

spider fragile & fragmented form
a brek-down donkey-cyart spasmatic
but nothin like the spider nor the donkey rider

each move i make you know the counterweight
if i dodge left i find you on my right
when i smile bright your teeth are dark as night

There was NO-
way to win against this double-spinning teef
and every tack i take you knoweth the brockade

i wither into stark ambiguous fate
i get some claps (applause) i fall down (woes)
like one high-rise skyscraper's pinnacle of cyards make out of bricks & stones

The more i farward w/the vision of my poetry
the more you bline my eye so i can see you better
the more i kno i dyin the more you kno i dead

So i lie prostrate on my chattel bed
 because you owns my head . and since i cannot sleep
 you fills the night w/ghosts & demons & the longest dead

and when & where i walk & use to walk w/smooth & grace
i now fall under the 'disgrace of fortune & men's eyes'
and along the sunlit library wall my bitter scarecrow shadow mocks me as i path

But these are likkle pretence rhymes
that seek divide the terror & chimera from the truth
the double-headed beast that owns me now is not diminish w/no tricksy verse

This is a curse of which there are no words
enigma cripple me & bind me blind me down to dumb
you hold my pen. cil sit upon my shoulder & nib & nestle down inside my liver

altho the light is on . yr dark is elder
and in the end you take my wife & eat my life & lover & make my bed
at last my grave and your sarcophagrass

<25 april 2011 . 11:05pm>

meʃon (1)

Each night now he hopes tomorrow will be better weather
And he's put off all his hopes to that beginning
Like a dead star at the endiing of its tether

<6 jan 2011 . 2:45am rev 31 jan 2011 . 2:53pm>

meson (2)

wil i be able go on scribbling these weak & comfort poems
lying here in bed until i die and lissening Sinatra Sunday afternoons
upon the radio until the rock of darkness come

the brown sQuirrels in the Park outside
are not yet back this season.   perhaps they know i'm leaving
and don't want to have to say goodbye that reason

i wonder what will happen to the nuts they stored
against the freezing weather?
suppose i had an aXe and chopp down all their trees?
my lynching block upon their life of tremor?

<17 ap 2011 . 1:14m>

38

"My labour is to collect the stuff and their teefin of it will become free labour for dem – like in slavery"

yr library of aleXandria - iT
- which has so brought you down so low so down – yr *cultural lynching* as you call
it – that has destroyed yr body & yr soul

tied in slip bowline knots – in six short six long years in yr kilombo oumfô
here on the metropolitan plantation
- what you have captured back from scars and slavery
- the middlepassage ship as wooden horse - and made you what you are
an avatar & ancestor . a burrow in the backle of our cultural khalam

But you gained no power no support no comfort here
altho you tried to 'access peace' as Belafonte say
- because there was no palinQue or paling where you were for yr protection
And so they get-in here to what you have and what you have become
- *teefin from what's really* **theirs** - is how dem see yu through these desert years

What you have nourished is yr poor man's grave
made for their free labour . as they call
it . and you slave

39

So teefin is juss tek
-back what you owe
dem. *nó*

problém. no

dis. respec my brotha! - the fungus fingers workin scoff & tiff across the System
of 'entitlement' knows no-no juju music bend . this 'cultural lynchin' as you callin
it . pay

-back across yr body belly-bottom & yr back - the cross across yr soul for being you
. whip
w/out wit and w/out end for ever having
iT

<15 feb 2011 . 8:15 amen

iT (MR) = infinite i-iteration – infinite touch on touch on touch – the moment that the golden mango hits the ground and what the ground feels back in return
– that *radiance* or *darkness* in-between – blind vision – origen>

40

to be tripped/stripped/fall/fallen
even as i swing into the last green slanting curve
of wind and final bell

To have this broken end. this un-
xpected un-
fulfilled. this saddening down-levelling

The rest is like the reel
of life passing you by. child-
hood. RH. MQ. MiEsse. Bob'ob/Ogoun

and the immortality of the ceaselessly-in-motion adolescent years
running running running running like stream through waterwheel. grass
along hill. slide. River Bay. the smell of breadfruit cookin. Mabel & Miriam -
the beauty voices of those solar sisters. my more strict family aunts

who want us to lie down rest beside still waters & not play an run-
bout in the hot black-people sun . who wear hats even in the closet
and 'Babes' who always flair her 'bobby' socks as well

They have this little magic house they sleep
 in - up on a little steep among some tamarinds -
Edith. the said 'Babes'. happy big-bubby Audrey Redman
old GreatAunt Hagaar Agard from Benin

And my Grand-
father blind . you had to kiss his prickly cactus face of hair
each eight-weeks holidays you come to visit in his rockin chair
beneath his photograph. O

how had William Mary Wordsworth loved these years. Cambridge @ King's
& Queens . the faerie sunrise castles of surprise floating upon the music
air . the liss-
less time-

stop summer punts by Caius. green water on yr wrists
white rushing sound of weirs. the spirits. pints. the swans near-
by where you wd later love her love her love her to serene
among the willows on the Royal Backs

These lifeline snapshots gone and now wreek ash an rats
because of how you eat my corn an lack pan me wid scarn
and teef my time & latitude . the so so many other likkle ways
you come-in here to larceny my secret sorceries and humming hoom

you nyam the who i am . you win the race i run
Only these sad desperate rhymes left now betray my pain
and all my strive forgone in vain

»Friends«

at the dark end of the stick

at the dark end of the stick

      my body gashed and broken w/yr blows
      blood over all my spirit and so spilling in my soul .
      for five years now this agony.   my mouth stale dry

      pain in the footsteps of my heart. walking me down this god-
      forsaken road .   all that i do i cannot turn it back. bones of my fore-
      arms starting to show white & shine like marble and as cold
      now all my flesh is gone

      i do not wish to say these things but must record them
      for the own narrow passage to my mind. still hoping justice
      for my lyncherers who leave me here beneath
      their tree. its splintered branches in the speechless breeze

each time i close my eyes i know i nvr wil reach home

      <4 may 2011 . 10:35pm>

CARREFOUR

'I have a weird feeling you are leaving'

The silent narrative of friends
at crossroads
- cannot be simple hear/say premonition

it is our human nature/knowledge
and the infernal curse & course of it
If you dint come

w/us by train . then you are waiting at the dusty
wayside station or on the slope
and gravel sidings

near by the arrival/passing/crossing
because we need this help to help each other's hands to heal
these broken vessels that we leave or carry

Words at these turnages . their carrefours
are not in any hurry harmony
- not for this long long journey

We have been totally destroyed
abandon ruin here
played out as if it wasn't happening

as if for us is routine sun
-rise shining in tomorrow's wind
& window.   when we are supping at the table w/this double

-horn & spirit-monster underthrow fe years
and suffered it in silence after the first bell's warnings went unheard unhindered
. like still-born . un. heeded . will not end

O yes we 'leave' – and soon
- yr broken friend
beneath a bitter moon

- the flying kite of work
& writing hand cut from its breath
& song

the more-than-paper-maché mirage image
now tangle in a tree or lying in the gutter
after easter gone

And on the way to church or chapel mosque or synagogue
the friends who gathered . helped
to haul the red bull up . happy

& clapping hear it roar
. now pass its sudden unxpect
-ed tatter tuneless by

Is not yr crossroad(s) they are at
- they headin for a different blue
& flat & singing angel shore

O yes we leave – and soon

But what happens to the turn
of spirits left on their wheel & verge
of final shape.   the soft concentric runnels of our labour?

What happens to these potter's poems
now unfinishing?
What happens to our manuscripts. the long yard years
and harvest history hijacked & uncompleted?

What happens to our health
w/out a healer?
What happens to yr wife
w/out her husbann after all that harbour?

What happens to yr future
w/out the rock of outcome?
the peepin neighbour's face
above the palin of her auction block?

What happens to the canefield in the hurricane?
the homeless children w/out welcome shelter in the wind & rain w/out a door?
What happen to the hoisted kite w/out its voo and anchor?
who wriggles w/its pain no longer climber dancer?

What happens to the sky w/out a justice answer?

Rockin-Engine Country Roads

Friends use to be those footstep tracks between the wooden houses
treading at the back out to the rustle canefields & the hills
and at the front to the slow murmur of the cyart-road's track
that led to church or school or market and the town

Later they widen out the dirt-tracks and whiten them with marl an dust
and still later wider for the limestone coral   .
To do this. they bring-in those huge high rockin-rollers
w/the big round front tooth crusher and the smoke stick smokin at the back

Later still they bring-in tar & gravel. heat & fire
each district section section at a time – red flags green flags & the rock-
in engine roll the road flat flat flat flat like the old friendships gone

where once we lived so close together .   nxt door to one another .
crush black & bone & overrun & straighten out & strangle now into the highways of dis-
order along the carrefour

<10 may afternoon 2011 . for mQ fillmore . rev DreamChad b/day 6 dec 2014>

friends

i will always speak out of my own convince *cosmology*
especially in my carême (my lynch-
ing – *how you skin my cat*) as I have learn(ed)
it - especially as i've earn(ed)
it – both the cosmology & lynching -
and will not turn
away altho you burn my body to the bone and blind my hoom to ashes

Why shd you say my sale & salt & sorrow is not
so and yet say you love me. can you not
hear my wounds & scars my face stuffed up w/sleepless fears i try to cover-
up w/in these borrowed walls . the what i thot
was casual but certain future gone . my course of history
so suddenly blown down . gone wrong . no metaphors accumulating in my song –

not anymore

But still i write against the fair weather dark-
ness coming on. knowing that i shall nvr see nor live to see these words   .
for me no Noah's rainbow in the arc
of birds.   and i bleed on from what i am to what i am become –
a toneless scarecrow of my father's rune.   And yet still mwe in spirit if not in blood & bone
and nvr faltered in my faith.   and nvr finish(ed). if diminish. nvr done
even tho deep w/in the miggle of this waste.   as in Beginning so in End

And yet my friend . you come in here an tell me that i lie an aXe me why i bother why i try

Phoenix

for a brief reeling moment i thot i was back
gone thru the throat of the door

like before

ready to run in the sun have all the fun in the whirl
like before

but it didn't lass long
the moment was wrong

or perhaps it was right!   If it cd have been possible
a wonderful miracle .   all coming true

but it wasn't

another unpleasant . no way no way to Mount Pleasant
and all back to black . like it blue

Sparrowes building nest at CowPastor

7
o'clock in the bathroom and i look
up at the Quick sound and shadow flutter of the sky -
bird wing bird body — such nervous tender agitation
against the slanted louvres and then the other —
both in silhouette

and messengers of soul of somehow starlight
tho these are creatures of the day
He keeping her his company as she picks a straw
they've left there in the hinges of the louvres and fly
off only to be back & back & back again for other plys of thread

When all have gone . they bring more here — these dry
& shed & discard treasures of the pasture. The bath-
room window is their transit storage station —

each morning from first daylight to c eight o'clock —
the busy carriage & the crossing — two weeks of it —
from c Jan 11 to c Jan 20 —

and now the window glass is clear & clean again –
no sound no busy shadow but the wind & sometimes rain

under the western eave our house – a nest – just like the weave i find blowing in the wind
& empty on the pasture a few blue months before - just after Xmas and the New Year's Morning

<2 feb 2012 – 2:42pm . for Wm S Arthur – 102 . Barbados oldest & most venerable poet. going to his rest
at the Sharon Moravian Church about this time now let us say Amem>

photos KB Jan 2012

LOSS OF THE INNOCENTS

Who brigg that wind into our sail like out of no. where as it were this golden morning
give the small skiff move   .   so that it scroll out on
the blue lips of the water hissing at the brow   .   the spirit in the wood

rising as we lean towards the water's flank & flash & sparkle
and our land of everlasting to the leeward
Ahead – the sound of luff & glocking as we tack – the wide horizon

of the wild atlantic - our hearts rise up w/water's heave & ride
to Less Beholden - the SouthPoint lighthouse still ahead
There was no skid of fish that day   .   the sky was clear of frown

the wind's mouth shouting loudly in our ears. the plankton knock-
ing on the curving floorboards of the hull. the rudder tingling taut
the skipper ridin the ship ship-shape on its careen all the way round to Careem Corner

Where did this sudden storm come from?
the blinding rainbreak shadow on the shimmer   .   the thunder hollering along the reefs
our bobbing wood and rope and wreck upon the water?

<27 ap 2011 . 11:35pm>

The sea is ours

. the sea is ours   .   the sea is   .
its tides toss sweep towards and claim these dark
millennial hours. edges of uttarly xtent

the depths too deep for night

its greem salt kingdom sweeps us out away steep down beyond our power
beyond the camber of the keel where it's too old for knowledge
the bone inside my thinning fingers running cold

. eye in its likkle shell of life beginning its first feeling sound   . then sight   . intent
far before whirls & breakers
. long before love   . long before sorrow   . long before loss & light & lwa   .

<Ap 10 2011 . 9:03pm . for Retamar and Adrienne Rich 'Diving into the wreck' and before i learn that the US Marines claim 'the sea is theirs'
as their motto. We need this poem set to music>

»She Poems«

Awona

*Y*r eyes reveal yr heart of stone

and the hard places whe they bring you up
food work survival. not even Revival

in this high countryside . even the Good Lord keep at a distance
It is the history of the whe you come from and alone

w/in the world of blame resistance bread . salt
and the chunk of red meat nyam right down to bone

The spirit languages of the tombs you speak . just enough water to separate the syllables
from flame . There is no love lost among the vowels . not even in the molasses of the Plantation

Nothing fe this cock-pit cock-fit country have no name until the rare rain falls
Grine is the colour of yr labour covered w/the pellables of desert and of dirt. The Sinkle

Bible that you reed don't heal . are agonies & lamentations. You don't even believe in the eyes
of the Prophets and the prickles of indigo straight down the wrinkles of their spine

Each word takes flare of itself & its passion & stain
and at night you are careful the cistern is dry an you don't waste the lamp of its eastern

How is it for you now you a-come down out of the mountains into the plains of deliverance?

. Even here . til you can sing Redemption Song . yu cyaan't share the pain and the dances

and the fireflies

sunday 14 Nov 2010 . + 24 feb 2011 after hearing Lorna Goodison reed it s @ The Americas Society (NYC) Symposium fe Bob Marley

At least it seem i write it so it shd sound

Sleep now so sad yrself so there . here in my arms
the fear & sorrow disappoint hold deep hold deep
and hides from me and keeps you safe from harm

<3 march 2011 . 12:33am>

And now Dear Eglantine

The cup lip chip.   She leaves

it blind.   Too too-much whip.   This firement too too much dire
imported on her mind and sucks her teeth.   How
to survive this all-very-well-for-you-to-say.   How live thru all this copperwire with-
out hemlock . wine . or salt . this open space of locks & timelessness & bells
hell(o) on earth.   like in rwanda poems chaucer's tale and dante's hell

She (XX)

allow the poem mek She leave the room
go to the kitchen check the pot the porridge an the chickenbones

find somewhere sit where is less 'hot' less pain
more/or less shadow better weather. likkle rain

She won't or can no longer share that past of you
that part that surely contained jump-up jouvet tones

– that 'Other Then' the Who you really were
not the dim shapes She now sees tinkling in the stars

- whose limitless dark whirling spaces
say more perhaps than any poems curl

We sail
. now we are bound together to two different shores

<Sunday 17 ap 2011 . 12:44pm>

Sleep Widow

yr wild thick tangle hair
O my career
to love you rule you rude you
the ramble arms now tossed across the sleeping pillow
black ovalesque & warning warner-woman agate eyes . their dormer windows closed
you soon to be a widow which unsettles you
And so instead of comfort we drive beguiling wedges
bull-fight like lock-horm logga-head until the evening pools the grief along our edges
and cools us to this peace

Sista C

She knows now that you dying
    and looks beyond it
        keeps walking on towards the light

<3 may 2011 . 4:35pm>

*W*hy is this alarm of roses in yr hand

when all i want is peace w/you across the waters and across the land
becomes you thru this amaranth-like red of love you bear

*T*he pool of silver star-fish swimming in yr hair

Dream fe Chad

ife . tree of my life

How can i tell you i love you so that you understand all the path-<<
ways leading out of the village and how the future will follow How
you will understand the wind coming in thru the pauses

The discrimination of all these various phonemes – the soft vermilli-
on clamour of flamingoes rising from the lake. Is it the noun at the
end of the road or the verb bringing you back to our home? How
do you phrase crossroads? How praise to thevarious gods in their va-
rious listenings? How to grow ears that will hear what you sayin?
lips that will follow the way yr sweet tongue curls so that we see th-
(e) same thing as we point to the trees and the last slip of the edge
of the sunset and the dark royal magenta island-shaped clouds pass
-ing north in the silence? the flat sandals of sound and the sentenes
they make as yu walk down the road of the village. edwidge. ad-
woa. What is the word for how yr feet walk on the ground?

And even after these passages. know that i cannot speak yr sculpt-
ure until i kno these forests like from i born an get loss & tangle-up
in the footsteps of their roots. knowing each tree from the nxt in th-
eir doorways of shadow & climb to the light in the distance of whis-
pers and the great silences and the shape each tree carries as strip-
ling or monument as now here forever it wd seem. or in the briefest
moment of their dream. And you see it even as you learn to speak
their miracle. even before you come to the land of the groves and <
the graves of the monkey-marassa. knowing each trail like knowin
(g) the tale of the god in the palm of yr hand. The speech of the <<
wood now. which as i say. is the shape of the form of its future. <<
how it flowers now in the wind and the shade of its shadow

But something is happening here to the word where it takes its sound from the wood. All these are new forms of the story. a yet newer monition of prophecy terror ugliness & scarification. ropes chains cultural lynchings howlings of amputation. blindings of the eye beyond its horizon. metaphors gone so ascrie i << cannot find you w/in them. The wind in its pain thru its pauses. i cd have gone on writing forever if this new world hadn't suddenly happen. How even the word of love changes on its leaf. turning the page of the blue into hollow. the dry >>> howl of the mouth where there was wonder & water. But two people together in spite of the Basilisk terror. Our nam still tie-knot in spite of the language i losin . is yr touch of me that still teaches .

ICONS & LIVICATIONS

Louis Armstrong   .   Teef of Sorrow   .   A War Memorial

a black bronze sunlight sound
blue shadow(s) slantin at the coffle corner
He shows no sign of the long journey
the thick dark ships . the narrow whips
the sweat-stain granate Papa face
the bulging eyes . the grace . the laugh-
ing angry lyric of the burning jaguar
successfully come-
Ova . the gotcha-by-the-jungular
and our great Teef of Sorrow

<4 ap 2011 . 12:55am . 26 april 2011 . 1:36pm . for Tom Dent and Jacob Lawrence>

The four strong daughters of the Bajam family of Dundo Lane

We've come a long way back from wherever we have been
We've come back home to be of help to Mother in the end
That's what it's all about . and every daughter says this cause she can
and can do what she can . unspoken . true

if is juss foldin clothes or runnin nimble to the shop or mi*X*im blue
or mekkin sure they keep the kept-in dog left out of fleas . collectin senna leaves
Because each learn their lesson in their diffrent pages up from the Mother's waist
from the Beginning . like standin up beside her in the kitchen . bad-talkin . shellin peas

helpin to haul & spead the sheets across the sailin clothesline . learnin to 'look serious'
on 'serious' days . earning the skills of cook & heal & hex & bottle-washer
the strength of body spirit sex & generation dat tek dem out into the spinning world
of wages as from this island most girls grow . not one a token

Standing now . a close tall louvre line of various colours in the Famly Digital just taken
such ark such art such link such hope such happiness such care of crystal crisis over-
come . the vase alive . not broken

.

for janice whittle
18 feb 2011 . 11pm 19 feb 2011 . 11am rev 21 feb 2011 to turn the page an let the other Mother Poems in . reformat 22 feb 2011

Corn-Rows

it's not the stuffed cloth dolls in view –
some of them black these days if still too golliwog – but that's not what

this picture bout – tho that is central too –
it is the seven little dearly belovèd heads of these girl-chilldren already six & heaven

What mothers' hands of skill & care & love this early morning dedication
to create these living Benin corn-row Bajan scriptures

‹27 june 2012 . rev 1 july 2012 . photo from the Barbados *Midweek Nation* 13 june 2012 . Lennox Devonish›

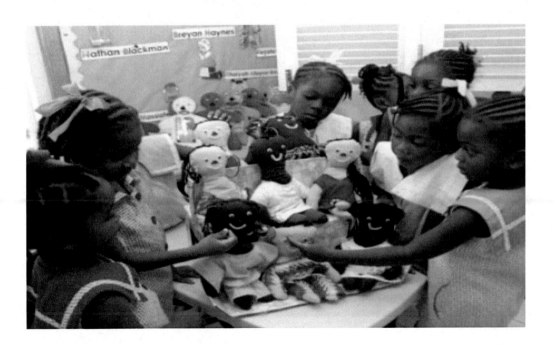

River Darlin

is when we wade out to the centre of the reverence
where the beach is . sparkle of lapis . o beauty of lazuli . the never ending end
of it . pebbles syllables swahili languages of sound

how the running running running embraces sticks silver silence speeches of light . delight

how this little island where we now are
the glitter of its reaches . the water heron on their stilts of slender all day long
becomes this darlin river song

for marlon . aika and frances-anne solomon

Kazungar

On one of the first new days of Spring . she opens the window w/her first-born just-one-year-old son of miracle who sits there in her love . against her body . the two together . for an hour or so they watch the setting sun and what it make . and i cd see the scene before me . the slow peace . the birds . the sky . the colours trav -elling   wide   miles   and   miles   of   ouverture   and   panorama

- and then she smiled -

'i guess he must have been remembering the day he came into the world'

<16 may 2011 . 1:54am   . for Dmitri . and Shelly Kazungar Escoffery . Chad's daughter>

Born

Now i am make made you

   from God was Dream but more than Dream
   the stream of life coming from what curvatures
   the earth beneath us blue & green . a new age horus
   full of grace now blowing from these distant shores
   you curled w/in the nestle where birds don't yet know to sing

   There was not even any thunder just the smooth joy of Spring
   that afternoon . start of the harmattan .
   yr eyes into my eyes w/ a strange cunning understanding and the sleep
   after like a leaf .   the rustle shadow of the feathers' wing
   like rounding the great silence of Havana harbour

   This thought . so like it was . beginning a new world of flesh
   yr earth cry opening that moment. the blind eyes seeing all this mist
   your mouth this perfect circle of such O . the sudden brightness from the dark-
   ness room you leaving. you coming back towards me . Time
   in this forest evening looking back and waiting for you with you

   love and such loveliness

Oriki fe Madiba

Living in this solitude
surrounded by its waters
whales conquistadores voyagers

Quarrying each day and every day
into the hard blind limestone blisters
of yr memory . re-

membering every . thing until it seem
like nothing. whirling whispers.
the art of how forgiveness is revenge

The engines of yr heart
work through the past & present
far into dreaming night

But you will walk one day Madiba
at last w/Zanyiwe Madikizela at yr side
yr hammer fist of stone upright

in triumph & salute into the blazing future
Even tho .   even in this iconic monument
there is no absolute

akuaaba

the black gaze of my doll
its glass soul looking in within
which the akuaaba does
not . seeking a third sphere .
her moon above the crossroads of the reeds .
She does not offer the Welcome her name needs

<28 may 2011 . 6:06pm . for Ayisha>

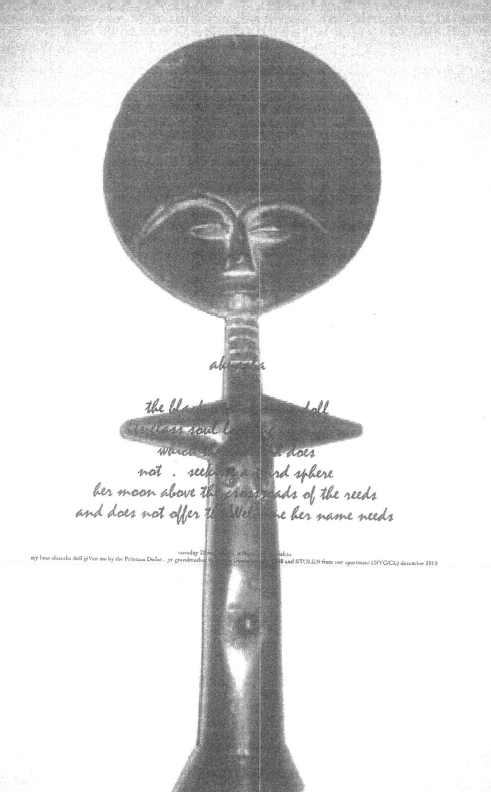

akwaaba

the black ____ ____ doll
____ ____ soul ____ ____
which ____ ____ does
not . seek____ a ____ rd sphere
her moon above the cross____ads of the reeds
and does not offer th____ ____ me her name needs

<sunday 22 ____ ____ ____ isha>
my lone akuaaba doll giVen me by the Princess Dufoé . yr grandmother ____ ____ Ghana ____ ____ 58 and STOLEN from our apartment (NYC/CL) december 2010

Sperrits

Ah! When the ghost begins to quicken
Confusion of the death-bed over, is it sent
Out naked on the roads. . .and stricken
By the injustice of the skies for punishment. . . .

W B Yeats 'The cold heaven' (1916)

Beech tree fallen among dreams

'. . .leave the stump of his roots in the earth, even with a band of iron and brass, in the tender grass of the field; and let it be wet with the dew of heaven. . .and let seven times pass over him.' [*The Book of Daniel* 4: 15, 16]

Outside my window in the cold

in its nether artifical necklace of grey bricks
an old beech tree upon the side-

walk blighted - perhaps by streetlights opposite
so that it cannot sleep or seed w/in the infra-red -
perhaps of lightning -

so that it cannot see the dead.   their dreams .
its blinded roots no longer find their way to water roses -
perhaps its age -

here since perhaps Minetta stream - the hang-
man's corner. the death-door dungeon banishment for slaves -
perhaps disease or heart-rot banging like i feel - who knows -

its leaves not growing seasonally green - nor fall-
ing - all the years i live here - twenty now -
among the whirl of daylight wind & pigeon flow

amidst the nightly planets & the storms & police sireems -
        it is cut down - down-fallen - in mid October Fall. the brown leaves
        going gold.   white inland seabirds clustering in shafts of flight -

        leaving a great new swathe of light & space
        at this round westem end of Washington sQuare Park among the young-
        er beeches . new place . new Park .   like so much more new light

Here on the pavement lies its stump its grave its epitaph
all in one turrible neglected jumble moment of activity
& silence & forgetfulness -

Those who come now - walk here - stumble a foot. step on the trunk -
wd nvr know that it once stood - w/tall & spread-out branches leaves
& sparkle shade & night-time dark & star-light peace & some-
times sorrow - and how it miss the Quick birds now

and how the Quick birds miss it where it was - their rectory
w/in the Park its special colour sensé place & contour in the neighbour-
hood's uptruding buildings tarmac tamarack & wood & water flow-
ing rivers through the flat silver marshes to the sea

       But here it is this morning - disc of the fallen sun itself
       its wooden wound - the amber colour of its wood
       become its face - dim when it is overcast and bright & golden
       when the itself sun comes out - like how this windy morning

       by the winding road - ancestral memories -
       its rough gnarl jagged bowl
       cut by the saw & ruin(ed) by those teeth - no
       vaunted circles on its plain circumference - no

       overt sign of pain upon its cosmograph -
       but quiet smoky grey stryrations - agony
       no doubt - but nvr doubt about its build of bulk
       the seismograph of wind & storms that blow here thru its history

       when she was growing up . her shadow on the ground .
       tho there's no sense of gender as we understand it. growing up .
       its stump stepped on by passersby who - as i say - will nvr know
       its history of tale & poetry - will nvr see its ancient song -

while she lies here - squats here - stands now alone in all her absence here -
- mother of her leaves' migrations -
aligning herself each daylight better to the sun and to the open sky

growing slowly back towards the next millennium
and all this time - in the cold falling wild - the sQuirrels tirelessly stop & thread & stop
& thread & thread again its golden tale among the living trees

•

They cut the beech tree down one cold snow morning dawn 5 jan 09
leaving the sun-face poem that watch back at us all that winter long
& 'remove' the stump in the late Winter darkness of that year

in early Spring 09
they 'erase' the stump & mark the sidewalk absence w/ a badly patch-up clay-coloured
irregularly constructed cement sidewalk scar & unpaved
grave

When the rain falls. amidst the mess & dirty settle sidewalk water w/in the ugly cement sQuare
.
if you look closely. there is a clear round bole-shape pool where you see sky branches
birds flying briefly by and parts of people walkin - their heads their feet their careful silent
torsos - and all in various ways avoiding the absence of the tree as they once did its presence
- and in both instances -

acknowledging

<9 ap 09 . 6:00am>

Poem w/out name or document

The Good Morning come into my room . inta my belly this morning
like the Good Lord himself dress in a whisper of blue
w/a likkle cloud and a gentle sublimation of breeze – almond tamarind hijackaranda

the nutmeg smile of happiness out there in the world
How is it w/you in yr land where there's this huge white plume x-
plosion & of fire. sigh jets too far up by the west of stars to betray their snarl

people gettin blown-up w/out meaning or while turning their heads to say something
and they nvr know whe they were . the huddle hospitals
bleeding & halt. w/out hope or the bell of salvation

Where's the sun by you on this morning after the full moon of silence
the pool full of blood into yr dungeon of loved ones. the little ones shell-
shark in the shadow of yr best friend's pieces of silver

i hear yr voice one more lass time like a creak or a mouse or a sperrit . a criss-
cross branch. a bird upon its vantage. and then there's no more sound under the sun-
light . the wound too bright for my poem

<20 march 2011 . 3:45am . rev 8:51pm>

Ogou(n)

Ogou(n) come-up into my mitan of the bathroom this morning when i am washin

my face & cleaning my teeth . the bathroom is the crossroads fe the *lwa* in this hoom .
they like the water the mirrow the shower & the wash-face bowl . ounsi owl

here some. times too
and Oshun and a smaller vershan of Yemanjaa because of the mirrow
and its silver

Ogou(n) come thru the pipes of the organ of the water w/my poems

and the organ is the rackle and the moan. ing sound of doves the old pipes make
in this rusty ole carrefour when you turn on the forests

This mornin im stann straight up inside-a me an straighten my back when i was ab-
lushin my mouth an containing my place in the universe

Im thank me fe entertainin the hungry sperrits on the Ides of March that long night
agogo when i provoke all dem poem-dem an im tell me that now i begins writin again <
that Oya my muse & my Stranger Companion like happy fe mwe - an the Ancestors too
- an how dem specially like 'revelation' (because of the NOMMO of course) an 'Fukushima >
Daiichi' (tho it ave too much *sword* *an noh likkle proverb*) not only fe Jappan an wha happen to
Hiroshima & Nagasaki already an how dem doan want nuffen like dat to happen again
an how it remine dem of dem-poem ARK an wha now gwaan wid dis cultural lynchin
an dat what i need nam is some ole iron inside-a my soul an dat banana might help an <
more carvival – *is that way e say it* – like 'revelation' an how e kno me all the way back to Bob'
ob an Mile&Quarter an Esse an dat i shd remember dat

in my option(s)[*]

||||||||||||||||||||||||||||||||||||||||||||||||||||||||||||||||||||||||||||||||||||||||||||||||||||||

Ghosts

There is a ghost in every anXious corner of this house
Some standin in the grey Quiet like striped wood Dahomey soldier *bocio*
w/no hands or the no hands waiting upon me from behind their backs
The unlit side-lamp by the bed is one of them

The midnight wings of birds outside the dark
And another one is sitting up and waiting all the while for me
They're in the rustle of the dust along the crevices of floorboards
Or with somebody coming back home late and coughing walking by the Park

The wet spot on the wall that i can barely see its echo of
or something i forget of love
The more i blind the more easily i can see see them
And hear them in the absent word the wind

<The Ides of March 2011 . 5:15am>

life soap

This salve of soap . new green and sweetly lather
upon its wooden dish

So like my life i watch
it day by day

a little less . a little less . a wish . until is just a slave a silver

<4 ap 2011 . 8:08pm rev 17 ap 2011 . 11:27pm . 20 ap 2011 . 11:19pm>

IMAGES

One morning glory when i go into the haunted bedroom bathroom
        there will not be my picture in the mirrow on the wall
        watching me so sad so still so hopefully so w/out yr help

        the ½ blind eyes asking why mouth no longer smiling
        but look now like a brief cracked leaf
        the brown brow scarred w/worry & w/sorrow & im. potent w/rage
        and wondering why why why me and no no no tomorrow

        One last night in the glass to say goodbye
        the dots of dust behind the fading rusting image
        perhaps one lass pretended smile . who knows . who cares
        there is no Spring w/in the silver . whose bathroom mirror is this anyweather?

        <17 april 2011 . 1:05pm and remembering Tony McNeill>

i come at last into the midnight house of my mother
for Sonia Sanchez

She hardly know me now. my Mother of the mornings

the quiet comfort growing evenings' heritage
is too long now. too late ago. too too much in between. even for her remembrance

She come because i recognize her nose. its little hook

where. in the nez. it has been pinched by her eternal glasses

She come because i call her. this last evening

after a short shipless sleep where no cloud passes

no slow horizon ending in mirage

My wife packs on. long into winter night. for home

even as i lie dying here no longer in the twilight. no longer quietly alone

2 jan 2011 . 9:29pm . 9:49pm . 15 feb 2011 . 12:12pm

Moko

For the 3ʳ time of

conseQ after. noons
this week am i visit
in my 'sleep' by the
Deads. this time it
is my father. And i
see his face. And it
was as if the One
who make me was
the Devil

i'm in this house. prob MQ w/the shop and the place is empty empty
empty Xcept for me. it seems. writing - occupied - preoccupied - in this Great
new Absence of the Afternoons - "You don't have time
for the world so you cyaan for. give
something back into the world"

i get the feeling th-
at he'd come in wh-
ile i was there w/so-
mething delinQuent
perhaps even dang-
erous in the atmos->
phere. i also have >
the impression that

my Mother or some
hounsi widows 'rep-
resenting' my Moth-
er and also w/out th
-eir faces since they
was all Deads - had
been talkin about >
him before they we-
nt out – had been li-
ke worried? or warn
-ing? – about him –
like moths or mother
  (s) w/a message

i kno that he had <<
come-in tho i dint <<
see when. He seem
to have gone into th
(e) Shop of Ghosts –
all that old Plantati-
on world of saltfish
& pork-barrels & ric-
(e) gushing out in riv
-ers from the silver <
trowels of the 'shop-
girls' & the white <<
sad softness of im->>
ported flour. flies ev
-erywhere sticking >

in sticky yellow to >
fly-paper on the wa-
ll and huge green tin
(s) of rancid butter
and the pillow rolls
of white shop-paper
on the long wood <<
counter of the villa-
gers on which their
purchases were wr-
app and the thick >
testimonies of all th-
ose bills of 'owing'
skewered on a hook
of wire & hanging fr
om the floor above
my father desk. But
something as i say >
was worrying me ab
out him as if he was
a dagger

And so i keep shi-

ftin my seat where i
am writing in the <<
gallery at MQ w/the
radio on so i cd see
what was happenin
happening if there <
was anything move-
mant or happening
and i trie to turn do-
wn the radio so i cd
hear better if anyth-
ing was happening
if there was any mo-
vement in the dining
room now empty of
dumplin & warm <<
spit-pea soup but <<
the radio wdn't turn
down/wdn't turn off
no matter how hard
i fiddle w/the ribbid
knob along my kora
fingertips and so i >
took it up & shook it
down up-sided-dow-
(n) to see if i cd see
where it was wrong
or anything like th-

at but it kept on >>>
praying louder than
it was before

Eventually i decid

(e) i better get up >>
see if i cd see what
goin-on And find my
father must have co-
me-in from the shop
an gone up-stairs be-
cause his bedroom <
door was cloze and
i newly felt him in-
side-there but didn't
kno what i shd do in
case e sick or some-
thing or that someth-
ing bad had happen
-in to him an i didn't
want to knock in >>
fac i v/much afraid >
to knock upon his >
wooden *barrier* in>>
case i wake him up
or something ohnfor-
tunate like that and
then . all-of-a-sudd->
en *there he was . st-*

annin-up on tap the
side-board table of
the dining room . my
short short father tall
tall takk up by the
rafters like a moko
jumbie . his head sti-
ll shape like mine bu
(t) too high up in los-
(t) aad spider-web >
to notice this

and there was like >
this contradiction of
the Spirit altho he >>
didn't say anything>
but was juss up-ther
(e) above me w/out
any sunlight or song
and there was this >
atmosphere about h-
im turnin him & turn-
in in him changing >
him changing him in
/to a something i cd
not recognize in the
red Quiet blinding-
me block & eclipse
of his transfigured <

Dogon face and i th-
ink then that i begin
like shouting at him
because i was afrai-
(d) nnd needed to >
defend myself again
-st the deep deep >>
well of space his stil-
ts became. collaps-
ing me up and i still
can't tell if he repli-
ed or not and if he <
told me anything to
my face out of the <
head of his languag
(e)

but i became more >
& more fraid some-
how & very scarr &
threaten . rage and
angry too . a whole

holy host of v/**miX**
emotion(s) as if i >>>
was goin swim into
some bright shining
choir of delirium >>>
and finally before i
burn/i turn & pick-it-
up this chair & halo.
hold it out towards >
the howling mitan
that he had become
– its four long prongs
of crucifiXion in my
heart . as if i was no
longer knowIng whe
i come-from in these
rags & tatters . as if
i loss the love i love <
in these elegguas <<
til it begin to rain &
rain upon me in thie
terrible bereavemen
(t)

BoloM

(1)

When **ROP Masks Islands** appeared in the 60s (1967-69) th-
ey was pelted by howls of the Estab Critics who reacted in word &
deed w/the notion of High & Low art – DW was High & approved
(tho diff). mine was scoffed at as too PEOPLE – too 'accessible' – <<
too POLITICAL – too 'poor'. The reeding of **Masks** at the Tom
Redcam Library in Kingston (October 1968) for instance – contested ov-
er – *what of the poverty of weather? shd it be held at all?* – xcuse
xcuse xcuses ***Problems*** for a night become so BIG it cd not hold
the Library had to be held **OUTDOORS** *fe goodness sake* – **li-
ke Yaad Theatre!!** - under the soff dark open sky - trees and <
their jasmine offerings w/out thunder – and **evvabody** there inc
yute and Rastafari and 'simple' 'unknown' women who brought th-
eir babies & their pickney but esp the babies for me to touch & kiss
because i was the spirit Marcus & the Highhead Bedward and their
certainty of Africa. is something that they did in ritual certainty that
night.   they dig it out from where it had been hidden in the

ear of earth. deep in the stones' resources. under the sac. red <<<
trees. deep treasury. abiding grace enduring memory among the <
yams - something they had been waiting for i did not know – this <
Night of Masks – for me to touch the child and give the whisper of a
name - Adjoa and Akua and Kwame Naima BuddyBolden Nefartari
back to the source of rivers

       i stand bewildered since i did not know this
       culture of my Caribbean. Those who rem-
       embered MiddlePassage and a home in <<
       Guinea. i had been sent the poem that i <<
       reed. They understood its message – ever-
       (y) tail & ital tramp and calabash oblation.
       Because i had been there and spoke the <
       broken & unbroken language of libation

Yet it was being said that the poem was *nothing more than a travel -*
ogue with a difference (Baugh) a one-more one-man blue-moon >>
rant – **Morant** - wannabé Rasta idrin. the manQué Madhouse pro-
     phit. offering the people bread strange fruit i did not grow

i stand here as the women an dem pickney-dem
to-touch my hand and kiss my cheek. It is their <
silence i will not feget. that silence of the night
of darkest Caribbean. that silence of the bare-
foot of the culture. where it so 'lowly' is. the pre
-sence and persistence of the *nam*. And *yes* i call
it 'certainty'. The child they render to my arms <
is suddenly so still. rest w/out wriggle. again th-
at wait & knowledge. As if they know how they <
had died & died to live again and know they has
to die again to live to love . to sing . to bring us
back

(2)

i linger once again in Bedward chapel
the high cathedral ruin near his house
in moonlight . and waiting for his plwé

He comes when music plays
in this old ruined palace . There is a shaft
of moonlight on the ancient floor. the tree-
foil shape of crack & barnish architraves & absent doors

No shred or wrack of glass
left in the haunted vestibules
The stone is white like moonlight sealing the revival halls

i wait for what is left of my godmanliness. my **nam**. my scandal
spirit gone and rendered from the aisles thru to the healing stream
. i here because i thot i heard the music that wd bring him back

And so i venture on inside this dusty
hollow place where on these moon-
light nights those who are dead and live near-
by are prayering around me reparation justice and redemption

songs . search-
ing for peace and love on bend-
ing knee and singing midnight all the night in white
as in Beginning so in End and wheel

<18 aug 2012 . 7:19am . rev 17-24 oct 2015>

reve**l**ation

Turn sideways now and let them see
What loveliness escapes the schools,
Then turn again, and smile and be
The perfect answer to those fools
Who always prate of Greece and Rome,
"The face that launched a thousand ships",
And such like things, but keep tight lips
For burnished beauty nearer home.
Turn in the sun, my love, my love!
What palm–like grace! What poise! I swear
I prize thy dusky limbs above
My life. What laughing eyes! What gleaming hair!

'Revelation'/**Sandy Lane and other poems** (Bridgetown 1945)

Sandy Lane/Sandylane is one of the most beautiful parts of 'beautiful Barbados' – probably an ancient Amerindian
settlement . and used to be regarded – the wildwood by the xtraordinary sea – as 'sacred ground' by all Bajans
esp the large black underclass. Some of my very early poetry & images are founded there
At the time Vaughan was self-publishing his pioneer book in 1949 (and 'Revelation' is said to be his Muse)
Sandylane was already being sold-off to (rich white) foreigner/colonial landowners
and today it is a 'no-fly' enclave reserved for them

Nommo

These two black bonded & unbounded bodies
are boded well & well beyond Vaughan's lovely
lyric
The majesty is here the magic moment monument
You stare while they stroll by beyond yr revelation

Such joy & doan-care caring

for margaret kawamuinyo . oshogbe & oshunide

in 1945 the poet H A Vaughan is just discovering the maiden daughter of the orisha
Oshun and she's already 'turn[ing] sideways' tho we recover herself and see her
'laughing eyes'. In this 2012 poem. the Nommo - Dogon Divine Twins -
have fully turned their backs on the writer
symbolizing that in the midst of the revelry they are already dead sperrits

and have turn their bscks to the culture

end poem poems

·

nd yet this lynch pass all these wonders by

no matter how i try to write-them-way like when the night sea
draw an leave mwe here still hangin from the swingin tree
It seem the Nommo and the martyrs – Bedward Madiba Lazarus the
birds - desertin all-a/me

Hurt has become a bad tooth stuck in heaven
What faith i had is strippin paper fallterin leaf
So likkle brief i had here on this earth
before this spirit-teef invadied me. this

deVil Basilisk destroying all thst i had an cudda be
Where Billie sing my bones can barely lissen
The grass below my feet is blood not dew-drop glissen

<19 aug 2014 . 11:10 am>

119

••

dead . like the cyandle flame guttering out

the last red wick . the brief white shadow . smoke
over the black namless sea. this
silence that contains no birthmark now . no life . no prophecy

<10 aug 2014 . 9:35pm>

120

My astonish avatar
at his altar afternoon

yr uttar sense of loss & disappointment
resulting in yr terrible depression
yr uttar sense of loss & disappointment
resulting in yr terrible depression –
yes that's what *you're* in my friend
yes that's what *you're* in my friend
and there's no doubt about it
and there's no doubt about it

And as he speak

i see my deep
i see my deep

loneliness

standin
standin
in a well
in a well
my own life like so far away
my own life like so far away

●●●

Sewing in Salt

let now my last robe be of this green naked shade and border
yr needle of embroidery rememberin the whispering edges of the sea

Moon

You rise in silent bloom despite our death behind our flame tree's bloom
yr silver curtains walkways on the open water of the sea
The scarlet blossoms of the flamboyant a moment blue
. If this is true . i love you . if it is not .
yr rising vision in the sky tells me i still do
How many times in how many hundred hundred years of happiness
this happens . two blue moons in one harvest & harmonious month . for you

. Dream Chad .

in august 2012 august displays two blue moons: august 1 + august 31

ABOUT KAMAU BRATHWAITE

Kamau Brathwaite, born in Barbados in 1930, is an internationally celebrated poet, performer and cultural theorist. Co-founder of the Caribbean Artists Movement, he was educated at Pembroke College, Cambridge and has a Ph.D. from the University of Sussex. He has served on the board of directors of UNESCO's History of Mankind since 1979, and as cultural advisor to the government of Barbados from 1975-79 and since 1990.

His awards include the Griffin Prize, the Neustadt International Prize for Literature, the Bussa Award, the Casa de las Americas Prize, the Charity Randall Prize for Performance and Written Poetry, and the 2015 Frost medal from the Poetry Society of America. He has received both Guggenheim and Fulbright fellowships, among many others. His book *The Zea Mexican Diary* (1993) was the Village Voice Book of the Year.

Over the years, he has worked in the Ministry of Education in Ghana and taught at the University of the West Indies, Southern Illinois University, the University of Nairobi, Boston University, Holy Cross College, Yale University and New York University, where he was Professor of Comparative Literature, and was a visiting W.E.B. Dubois fellow at Harvard University. He lives in CowPastor, Barbados.

Every effort has been made to secure permission to reproduce images.
The photograph on page 81,'Nelson Mandela', appears courtesy of Topham Picturepoint.